Table of Contents

Prologue 2

Mud Map Marree to Algebuckina 3

Beltana Station 4

A One Day Old Baby Camel 5

Loading the Camel Train at Marree 6

Camel Train on the Road North 7

Beresford Mound Springs 8

Algebuckina Waterhole 9

Algebuckina Railway Bridge 10

Coward Springs Hotel 11

Coward Springs "The Bubbler" 12

The Railway Over the Finke River 13

Oh...No! Not Again... 14

Laying the last Rails at Alice Springs 15

The Alice Springs Railway Station, 1930 16

Well-- Not Quite the Last Rails 17

Camels After 1930 18

Peter Mahomet and Family 19

Not Camels—Mules 20

More Mules 21

Poepples Corner 1 22

Poepples Corner 2 23

Todd Street Alice Springs 1929 24

Thank You 25

Prologue

The Australian Outback and a million feral Camels are not really getting on very well these days.

Thousands of the two main species of Australian feral camels, mostly Dromedaries but also some Bactrian Camels, were imported into Australia during the 19th century for transport and construction as part of the colonization of the central and western parts of Australia.

Look at these figures on their numbers and impact in 2009:

As of 2009, the feral population numbered about one million, with a doubling time of about nine years. Although their impact on the environment is not as severe as some other pests introduced to Australia, camels ingest more than 80% of the plant species available.

Degradation of the environment occurs when densities exceed two animals per square km, which is presently the case throughout much of their range in the Northern Territory.

Environmental degradation is not the only damage they cause; stock fences are destroyed by the mile, stockyards smashed, and watering facilities trashed, all in their search for water and feed.

These effects are felt particularly in Aboriginal and other remote communities where the cost of repairs is prohibitive.

At different times, in different areas, the Australian authorities have planned to eradicate as many as several thousand camels to ease the pressure on communities.

Way back in 1948, at Erldunda Station in the Northern Territory, owned by Sydney Staines, the aboriginal head stockman Alex Barney's main job was to take the Jeep and a .303 rifle, and shoot as many camels as he could, and that usually amounted to several hundred each week.

Syd Staines had seen too many miles of stock fencing flattened.

However, it should be acknowledged that the forebears of today's camels performed major work in the development of the interior of Australia. Today's troubles stem from that same work which opened up Australia to Rail and heavy wheeled traffic.

The work was finished and there was little demand for Camel Trains, so the animals were released in the desert country to fend for themselves.

They did so well that they are now posing an environmental problem.

One of the Camel Trains major achievements was the construction of the Northern Railway line from Marree in South Australia to Alice Springs in the Northern Territory. They would cart ten to twelve ton loads regularly, managed by expert handlers imported from Afghanistan.

This was completed in 1930, 4 years before the Government Road Train arrived on the scene.

The South Australian Government had commissioned the building of several diesel powered, 130HP, 8 wheel drive prime movers, each towing two, four wheel drive, self-tracking trailers. The drive to, and between the trailers, was by universally jointed drive shafts. They were supposed to build the railway, but arrived too late. The camels had beaten them to it!

Mud Map Marree to Algebuckina

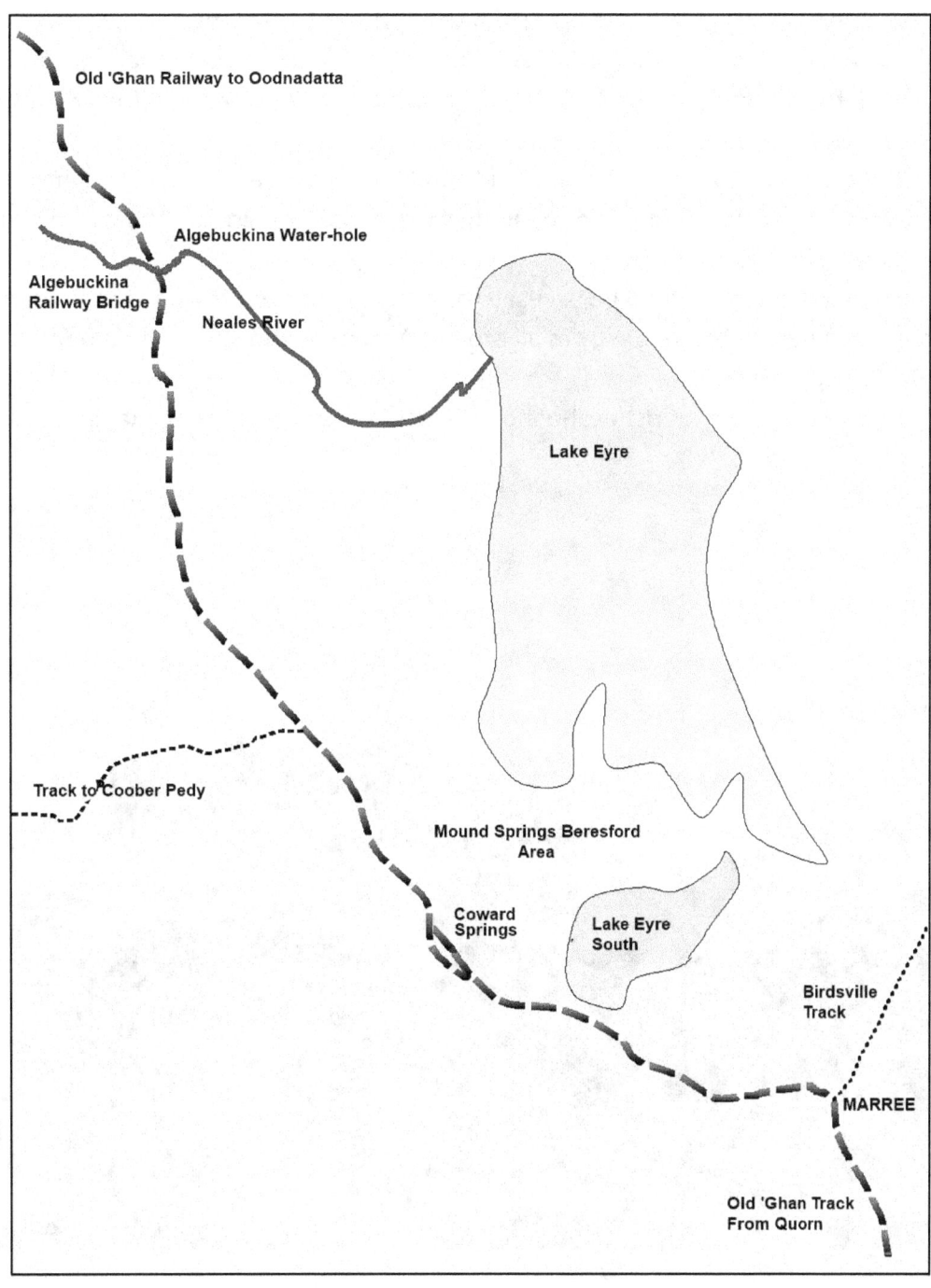

Beltana Station

Beltana Station, in the Flinders Ranges of South Australia, was acquired in 1862 by Sir Thomas Elder, and became one of the first Camel breeding and training enterprises in Australia.

The photo below shows the original homestead and a memorial to Ernest Giles commemorating his expedition in 1875 to Western Australia. Giles had obtained his camel team from Beltana Station.

Beltana, the town, is 540 km north of Adelaide and 240 m above sea level. Originally settled in the 1850s and 60s, it is hard to imagine today that the little town grew to boast a population of 390 with 70 houses by 1883.

Visitors to the town today could be excused for thinking that the town is abandoned, but any buildings there are owned by people from all around Australia, and they will be reminded of this fact by all the "Keep Out" signs.

Beltana Station today is a tourist destination. Camel tours of the Flinders Ranges arranged.

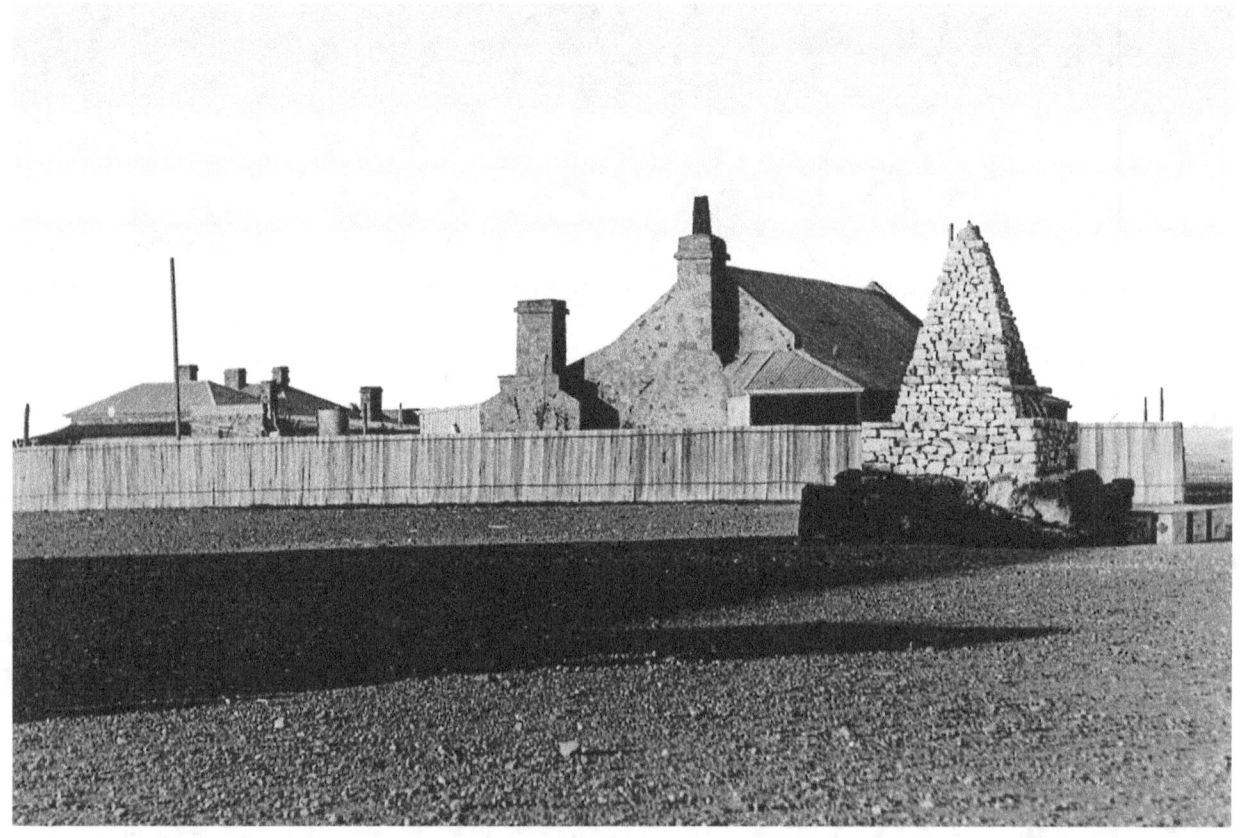

A One Day Old Baby Camel

Here's one of the Breeders on Beltana, after birthing a calf, with two station hands helping out. This is an example of the more common breed Camelus dromedarius, the dominant species of the Australian feral camel. This photo was taken in 1929.

When the camel trains were broken up in the 1930's, the camels were turned loose in the Australian outback where they thrived. There are now about 1 million feral camels which are causing a lot of damage to fences and stock watering points. It has been estimated that the camel population can double itself very nine years.

The authorities conduct culling drives to keep the numbers down to a reasonable figure.

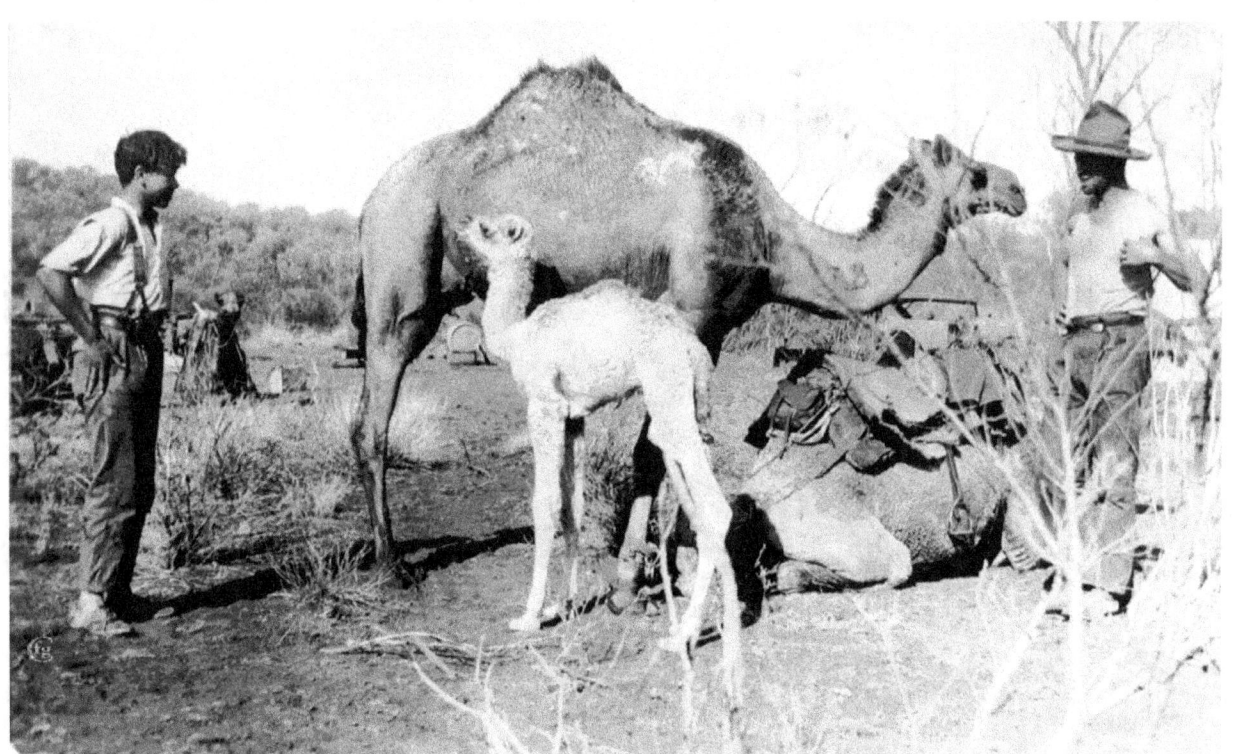

Loading the Camel Train at Marree

Marree, originally called Hergott Springs, the name being changed in 1918 due to anti German feelings after the first world war.

The northern railway from Adelaide reached the town in 1883, and Marree became a major railhead for the cattle industry.

The railway then continued north from the town to Alice Springs, and completed in 1929 solely by Camel Trains, carting equipment and supplies from Marree

The Camel handlers were mostly Afghans, 'specially brought to Australia for their expertise in handling the animals, and the train that travels the route today is named "The Ghan" (Please Remember! Pronounced gan, not garn!), in their honor, even though the route today is totally different from the original.

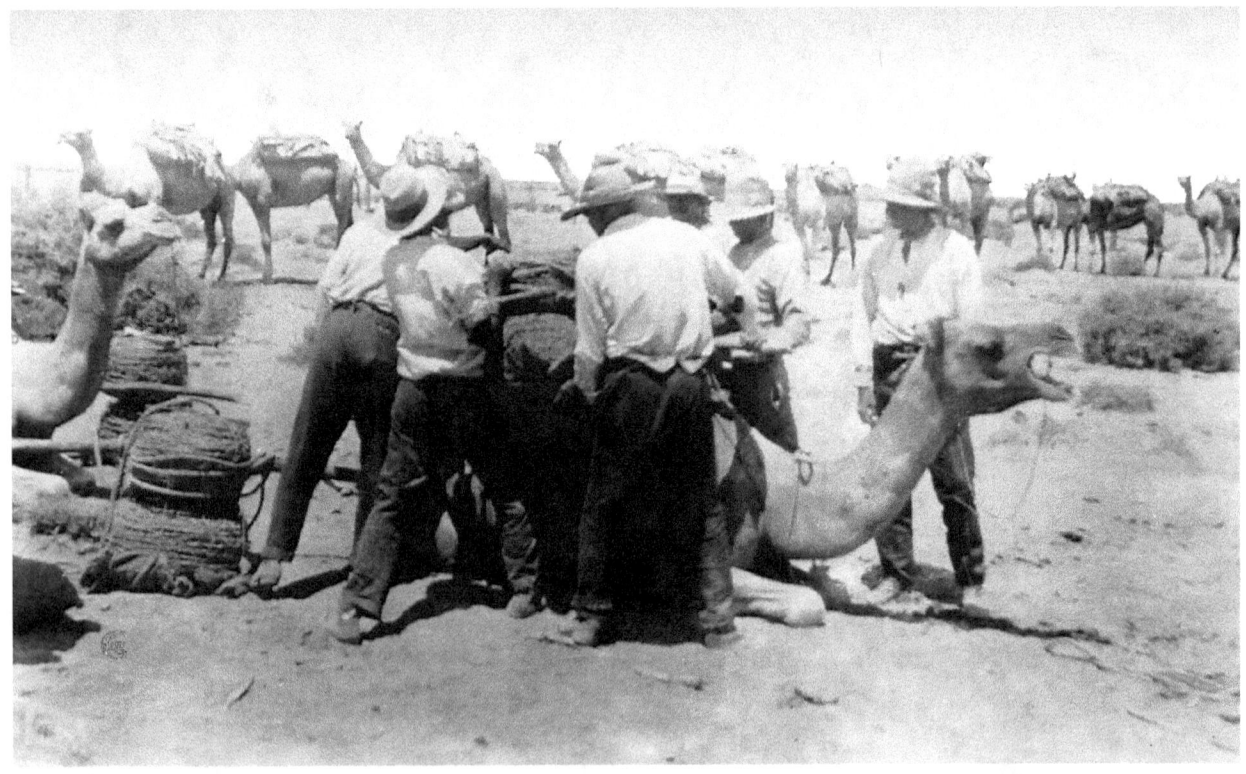

Camel Train on the Road North

There were enough camels to make up 2 camel trains, plus spares, usually one camel train was returning empty to Marree as the other fully laden one was already on the road, heading north towards Oodnadatta.

This Camel Train is heading north from Marree to the Head of the Line with more Sleepers, Rails, Fishplates, Spikes and nut & bolts for the new northern Railway to Alice Springs.

Look at the loads these animals are carting. At least 6 Sleepers balanced by a crate of iron fishplates and spikes, Barrels of water and rations, Lengths of Rail, balanced by more hardware.

Camel Trains played a major role in the opening up of the Centre of Australia.

Until the Railway was finished, no major heavy machinery, bulk fuel, building supplies or foodstuffs could be brought in. The railway was finished in 1930, and it wasn't until 1934 that the first diesel powered Road Train made the trip to the Alice.

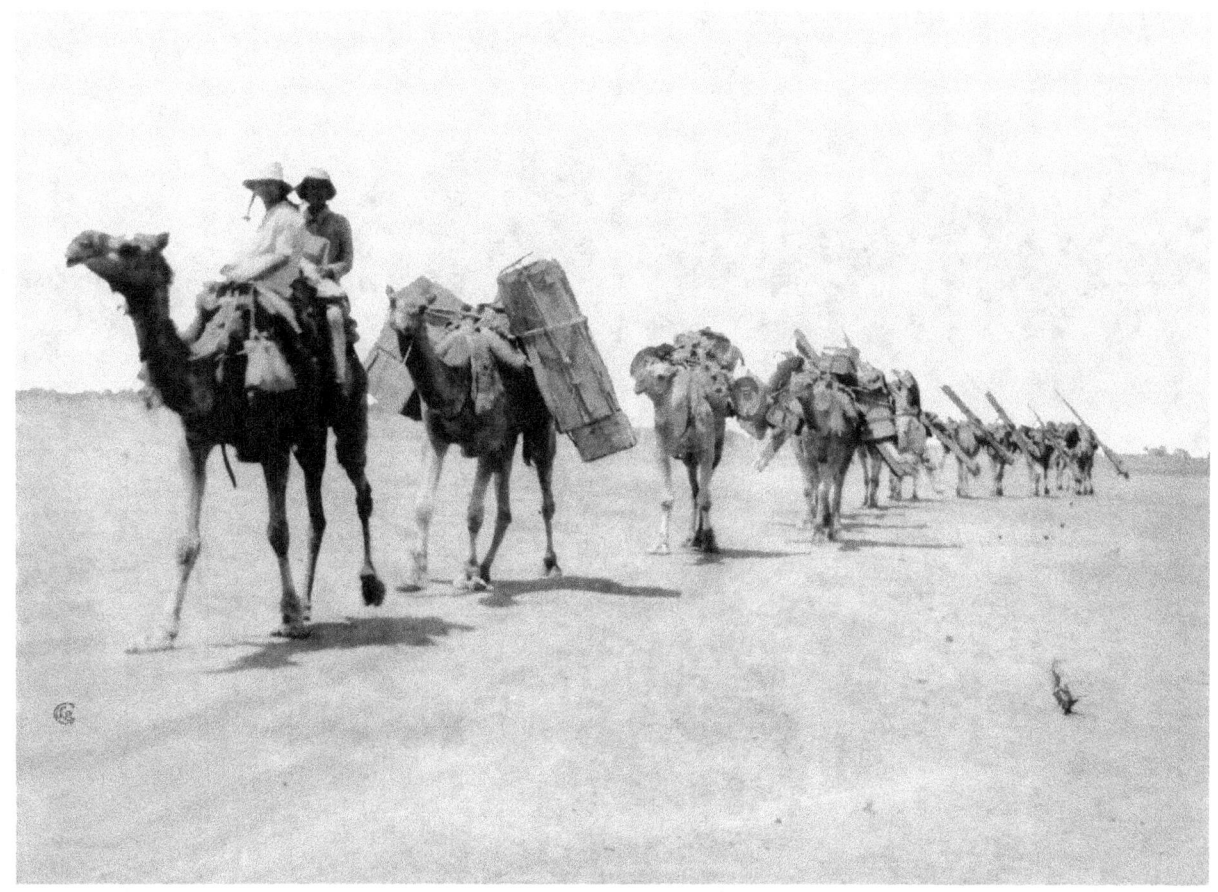

Beresford Mound Springs

One Watering point for the camels was at Beresford, where the Mound Springs had permanent pools of fresh water right in the top of the mound, which was formed as drift sand built up on the wet sides of the mound. Some mound springs that no longer flow are estimated to be 45 meters above ground level, and 130,000 years old.
 (http://digital.library.adelaide.edu.au/dspace/handle/2440/49737)

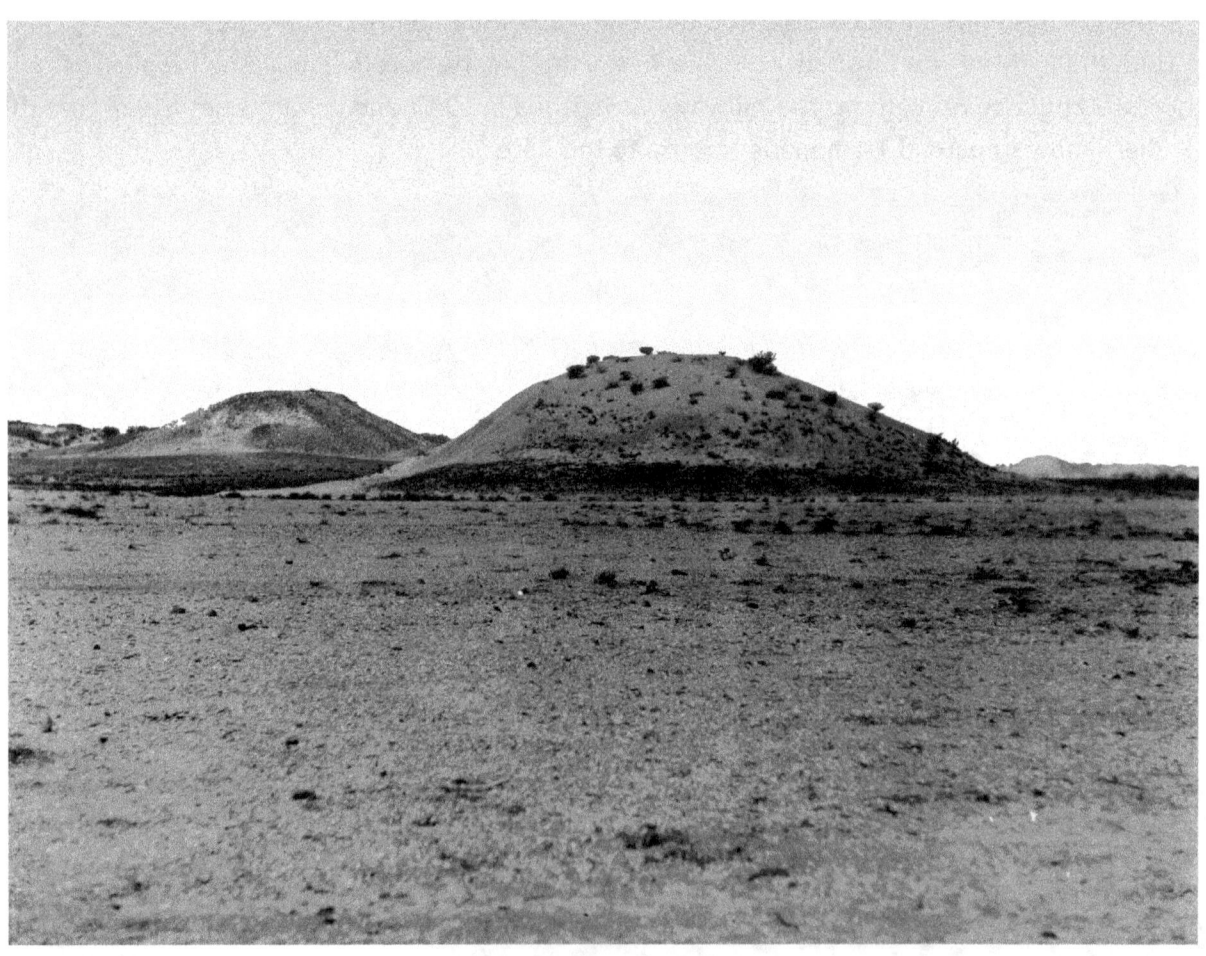

Algebuckina Waterhole

Another waterhole was the Algebuckina Water hole in the Neales River, downstream from the Railway Bridge which can be seen in the distance.

This photo shows the waterhole as a very small inter-connected string of holes, but…

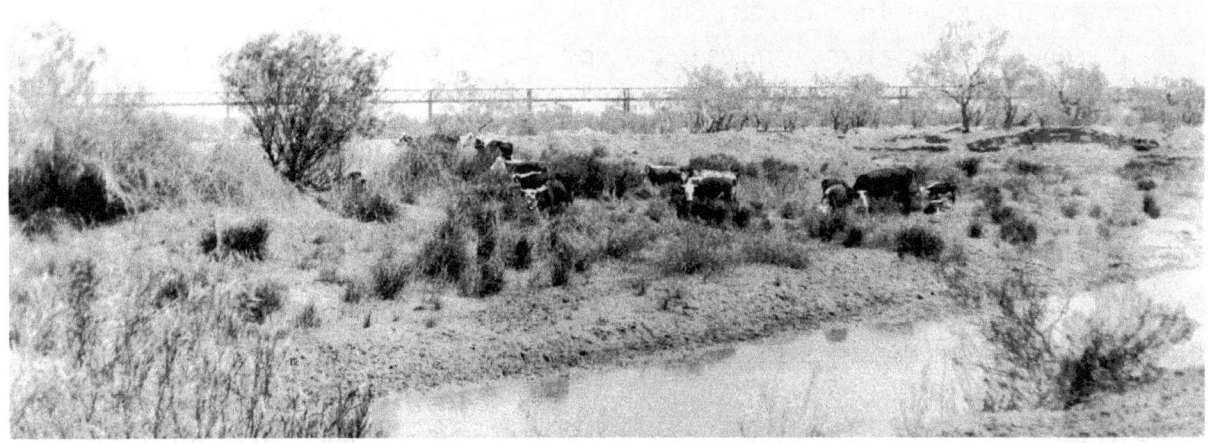

…after a flood, those cattle you see on the bank of the waterhole, would be 15 feet under water.

Algebuckina Railway Bridge

The Algebuckina Railway Bridge over the Neales River was built in the 1890's when the camel trains had got the line to Oodnadatta 40 mile to the north. The Neales could flood for several weeks at a time and could spread out to a mile in width.

Just over 580 meters in length, the Algebuckina was often used by motor vehicles to cross the flooded Neales. Passengers in the old steam powered "Ghan" would sit up until late at night for the crossing of the bridge. The 'Clacketty Clack' seemed to go on forever.

The present day railway is many miles to the west, but the track which follows the old railway line up from Marree is fairly good, and a visit is well worth the trip. You can't drive over the bridge any more as they've barricaded both ends.

After visiting Algebuckina, (the name comes from the Aboriginal name of the waterhole in the previous photo) you have a choice of continuing on to Oodnadatta, or turning onto the road to Coober Pedy, where you pick up the bitumen highway to Alice Springs.

The bridge is worth a trip as it is truly awe inspiring. Built at a total cost of £60,000 by contractors, sub-contractors and passers-by, one wonders what the cost would be today.

The figure, showing off, standing on the superstructure of the bridge is Bob Rumball, just as a

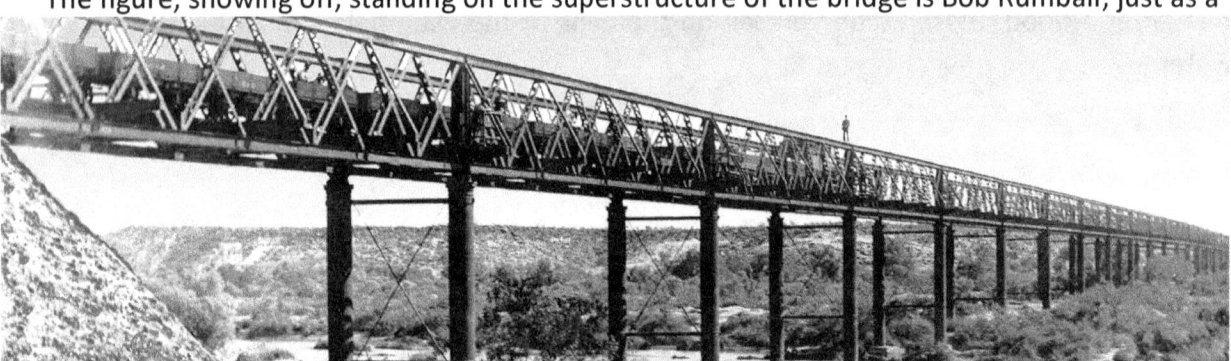

goods train was crossing it.

If you look closely you'll also see a few free-loaders in an open freight car over the second span of the bridge.

Coward Springs Hotel

The Camel Train returning to Marree from Oodnadatta stops at the Coward Springs Hotel for a cool 'lemonade.' Behind the Hotel are the actual springs, locally called "The Bubbler", where a beautifully clear pool of fresh water has this huge permanent bubble of water breaking the surface.

The pool is some 20 to 30 feet in diameter, and over 7 feet in the middle, or it used to be. Now it has been enclosed and nowhere near as interesting.

This photo was taken from where the railway tracks were, and when the old steam Ghan stopped for water, the passengers would race over to the springs for a dip.

Thinking to cash in on "The Bubbler," the hotelier began building a block of Units alongside the pub. They were never finished. And then the railway was moved several hundred kilometers west and the camel trains had long since gone.

There were no more people coming around.

So sad, as I have many fond memories of travelling home from boarding school in Adelaide, with dozens of kids from other boarding schools, staying up late to enjoy the passage over the Algebuckina Bridge, and the cooling dip in "The Bubbler".

Marty O'Loughlin, the train's chief steward, and "Aspro," his assistant seemed to enjoy these trips as much as anyone else.

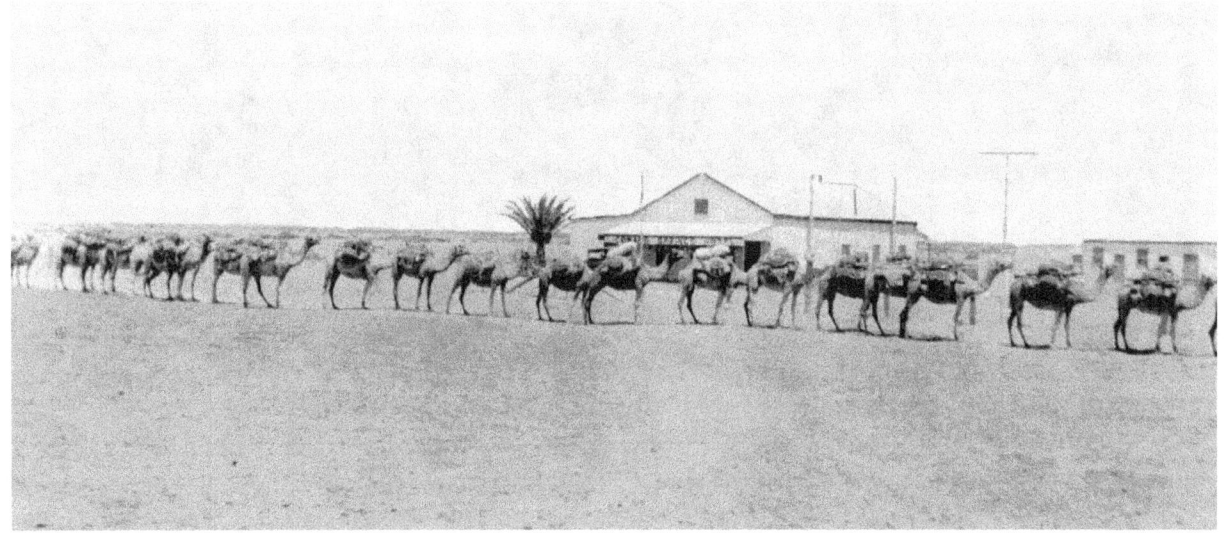

Coward Springs "The Bubbler"

Back in those days, life was fairly laid back, 'specially in the bush, and when the steam loco had finished taking on water and hooked up again, the engineer would give a couple of whistles, and the train would start moving slowly. Of course this created panic amongst the swimmers, and they would stream over the sand-hill to catch up with the slow moving train, trying to jump on board while it was still moving.

Marty and Aspro would be standing on the carriage steps and pushing those off, with a broom, who were trying to climb on board. Of course the engine driver was in on the joke and maintained a slow jogging pace for a while.

I don't think any of that would be allowed to happen today, "Ahhhhhh".... (a long sigh).

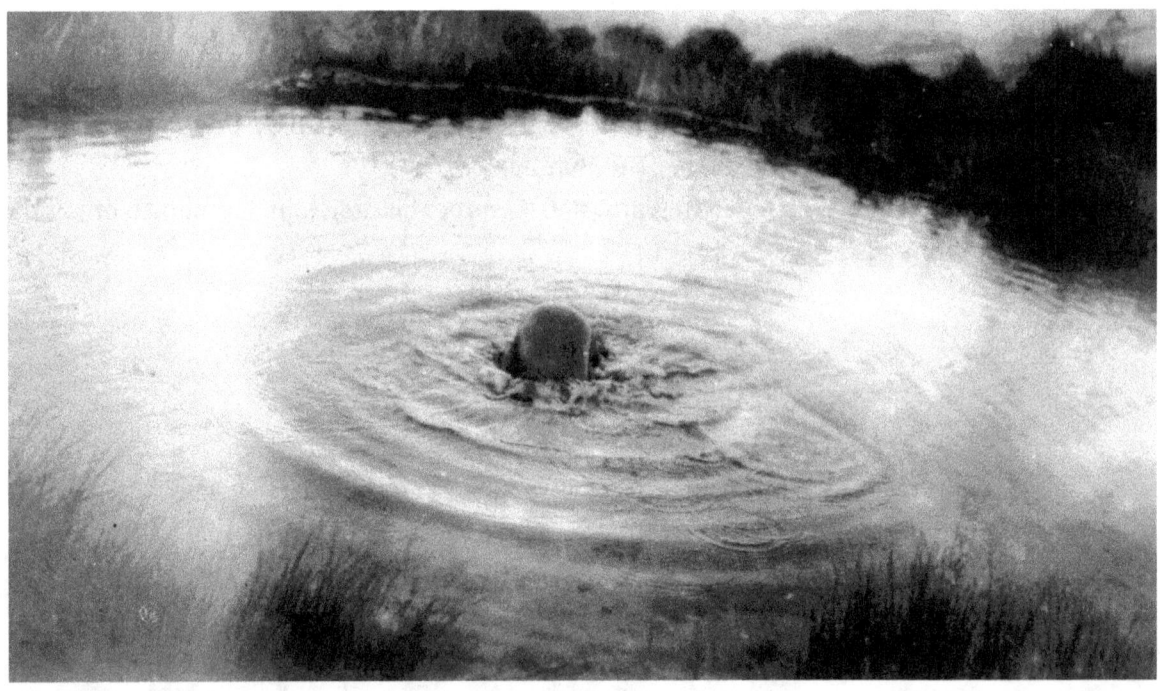

That's Progress?

The Railway Over the Finke River

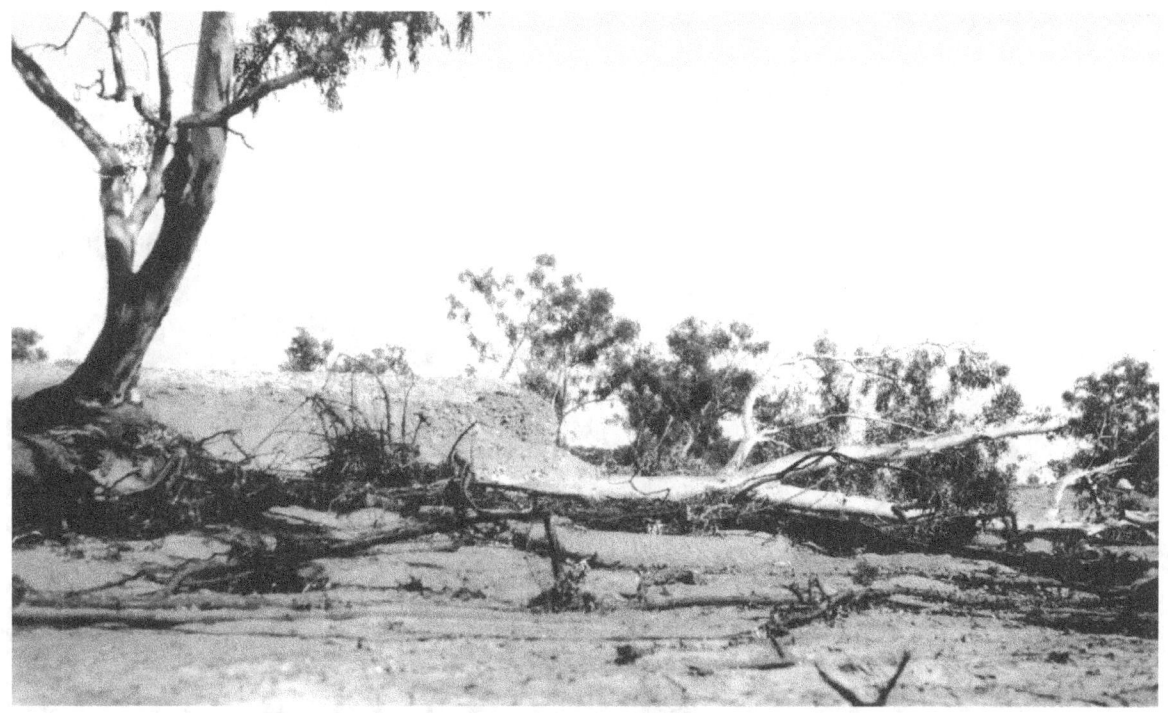

The bridge engineers intended to build a bridge over the Finke, and attempted to drive pylons down to bed-rock. The skin friction with the sand stopped them from driving them any further, and they still were not on bedrock.

But they went ahead and built the bridge anyway.

One goods train crossed the Finke, then a flood came along, released the skin friction, and the pylons sank until the flood waters took the bridge away completely.

The rails were then just laid on the sand, and replaced many times.

Oh…No! Not Again…

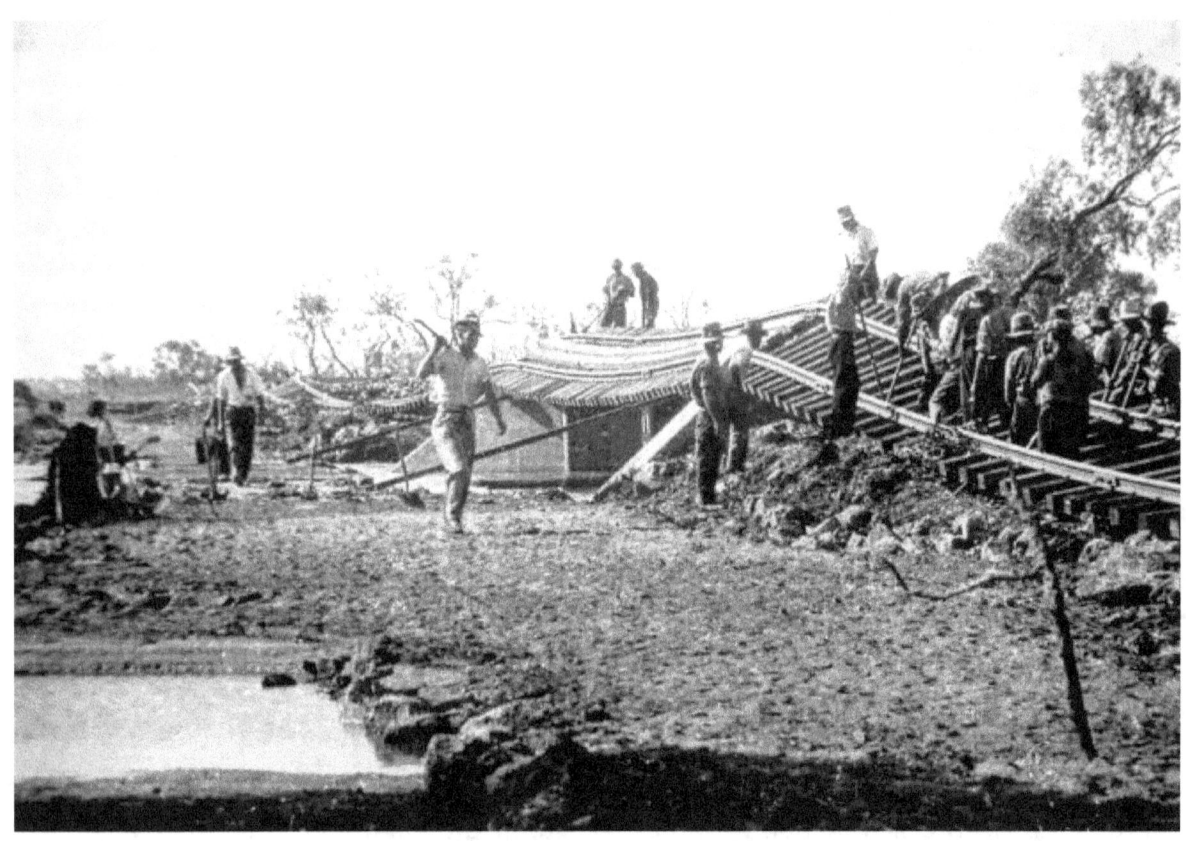

Eventually they did the job properly, but didn't make the watercourse wide enough.
Yep! I always reckoned they shoulda' built another Algebuckina over the mighty Finke River.

Laying the last Rails at Alice Springs

Late in 1929 the last rails were laid at the spot where the railway station would be built. It was a magnificent achievement for the Camel Trains and their Afghan handlers.

By 1930, passengers were enjoying the thrill of rocketing along the narrow gauge railway from Adelaide, the two nights in the sleeping cabins and the marvellous attention of the stewards.

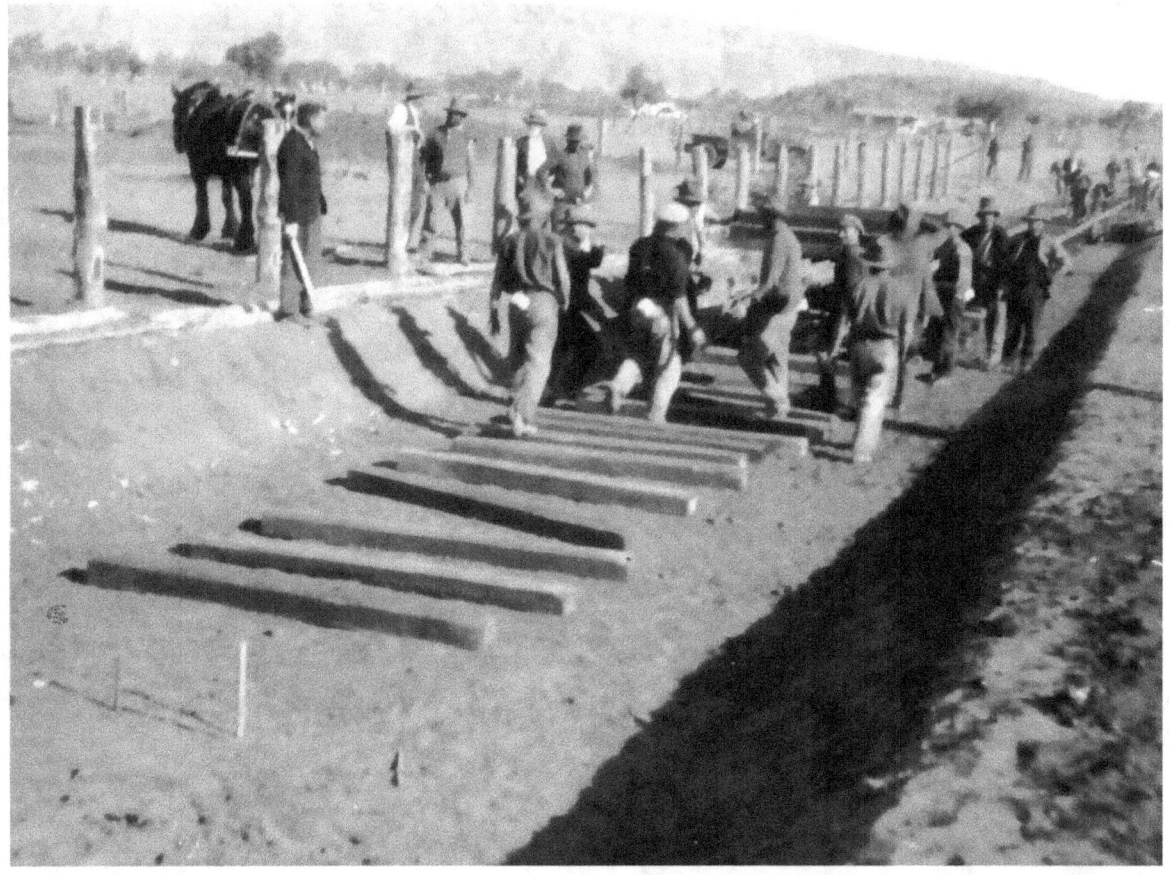

Of course, it's much different today, the line has been moved many Km's to the west, but the landscape hasn't changed that much.

But what a shame they didn't move the Algebuckina Bridge too!

The Alice Springs Railway Station, 1930

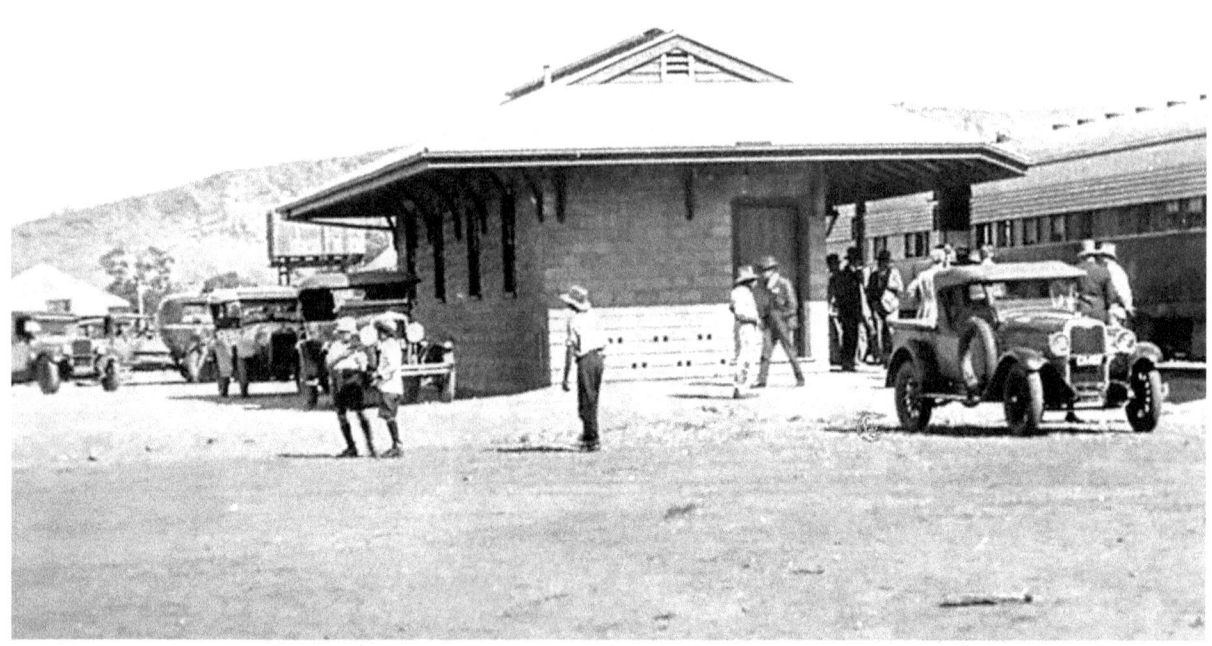

The first passenger train to arrive in Alice Springs at the brand new railway station. There was always a crowd of locals to meet the "Ghan" when it arrived once a week. The crowd grew as the town grew.

Well-- Not Quite the Last Rails

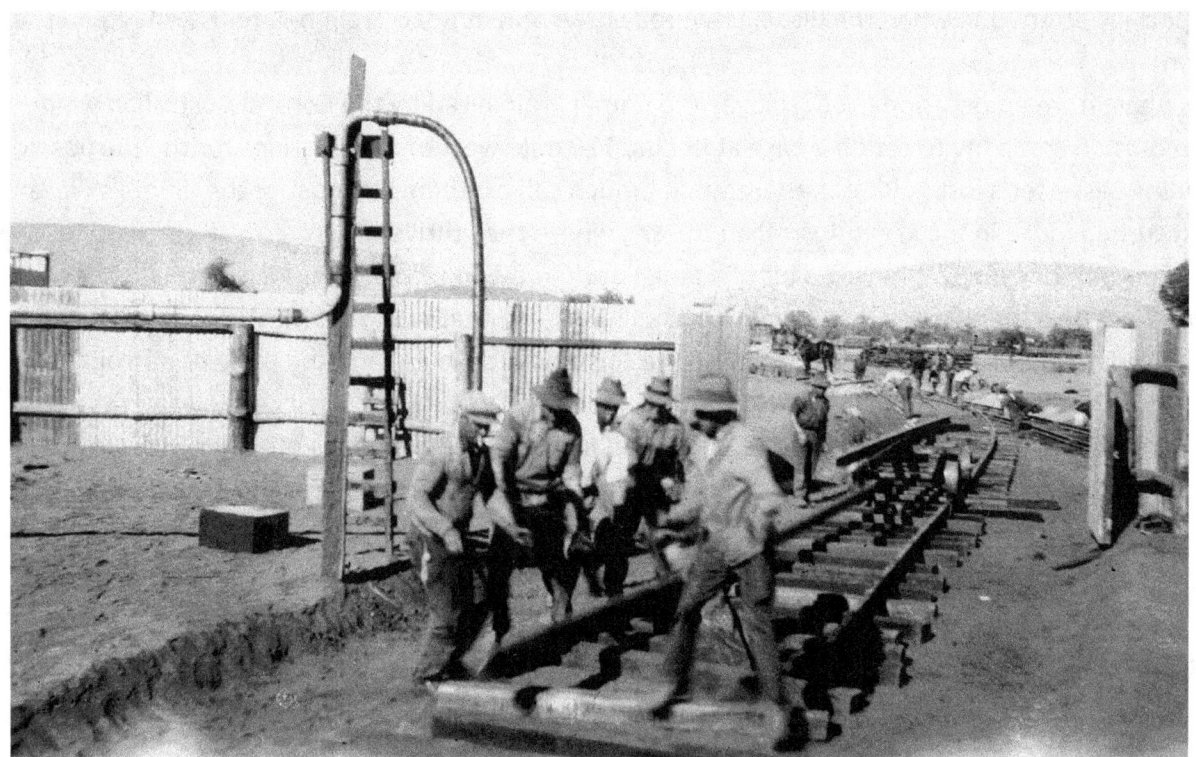

This was the real end of the rail in Alice Springs; the Rail Tanker unloading bay in the back of the Shell Depot where the fuel was pumped from the Tanker into various underground tanks.

The line shown continuing past the branch-line finished at a dirt ramp where cars and small trucks were driven off the flat-top rail-cars.

And that's where the railway stopped for over 70 years, before it was extended nearly to Darwin.

Camels After 1930

After the Railway line to the Alice was completed there wasn't a lot of work for camel trains, especially after 1934 when the diesel powered Government Road Train belatedly arrived on the scene.

Apart from an occasional job, such as the Camel Train hired by the Central Australian Gold Exploration company to set up a base at Ilbilba, 120 mile west of Alice Springs for the purpose of finding Lassetter's lost gold reef, there wasn't much call for them, so most of the animals were just turned loose in the great Australian Desert, where they thrived.

This pair of camels is having a bit of a laugh at the new fuel bowser in Alice Springs. They didn't need anything more than a bellyful of spinifex, and that was free. Maybe today, with hundreds of thousands of camels roaming the Australian outback, and the price of petrol, we should all be driving around in camel carts.

This is the Reverend Kramer of the Australian Inland Mission, and his off-sider Dick Gillen, checking out the first petrol bowser in Alice Springs, at Phil Windle's Garage in Todd Street.

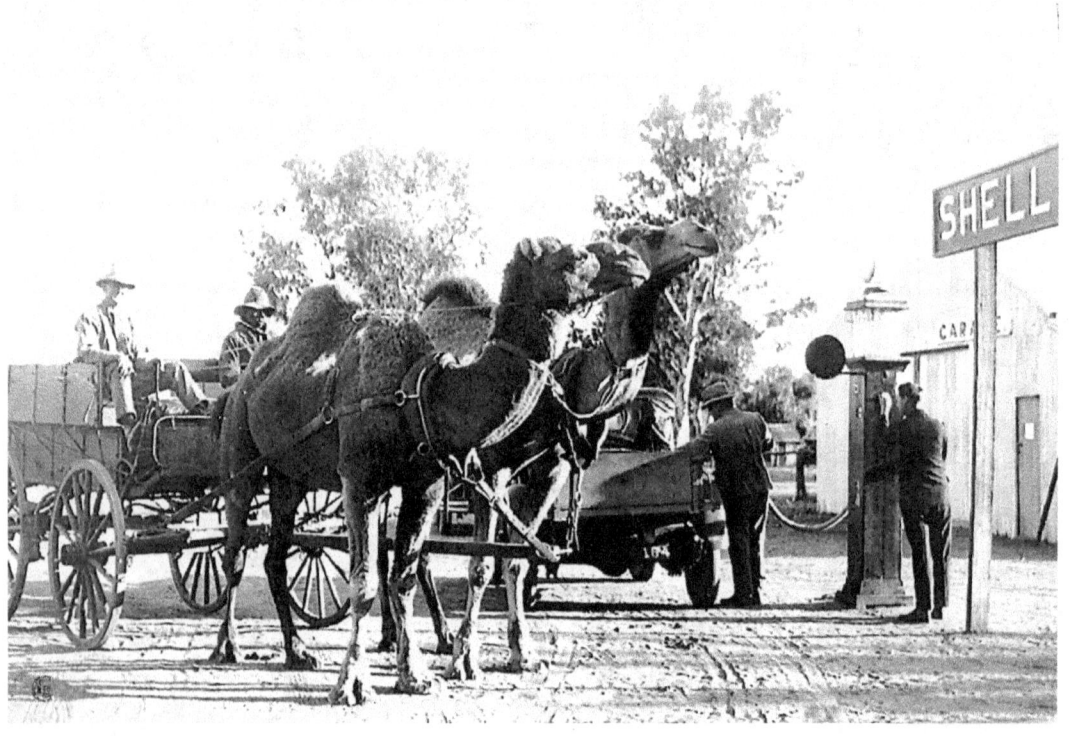

Peter Mahomet and Family

Peter Mahomet, in the photo below was a descendant of the early Afghan camel handlers, and he used camels to draw fresh water from his well in Alice Springs for sale to the townspeople. This is called a "Camel Whip."

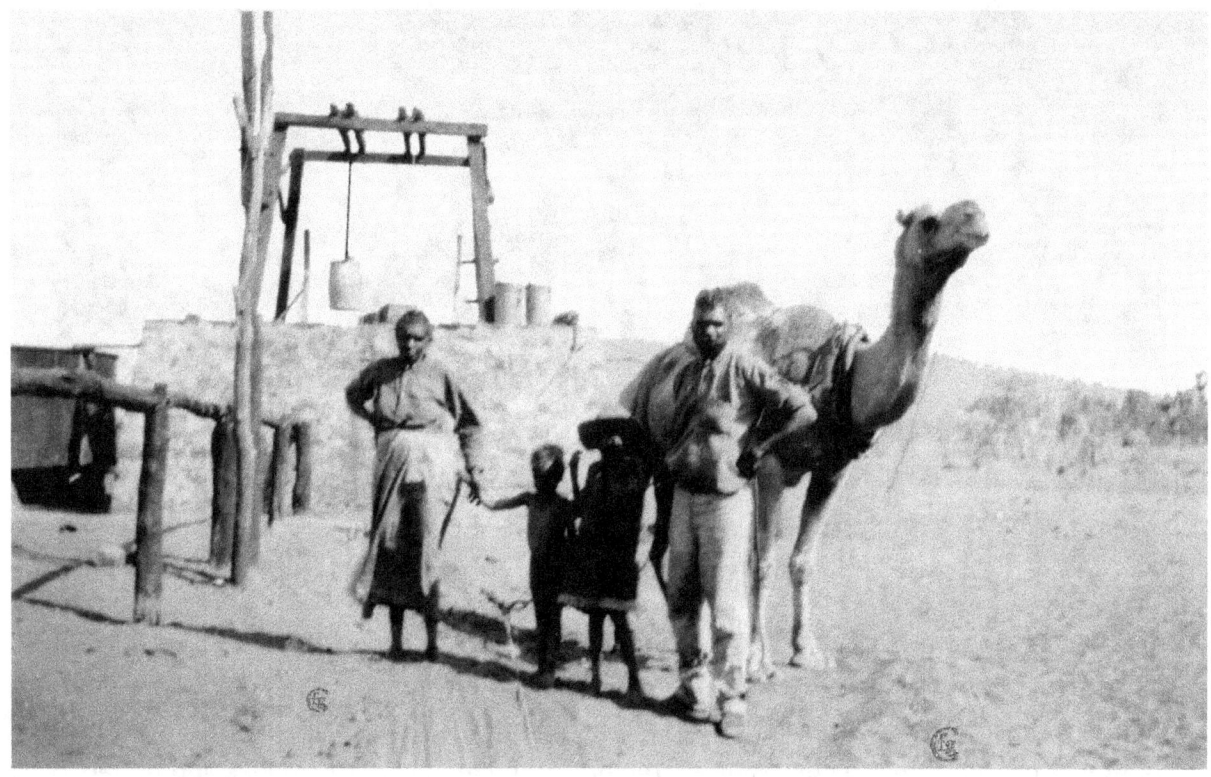

The little bloke holding his mothers' hand is a very young Ghul Mahomet, who grew up to become a well-known local identity.

Not Camels—Mules

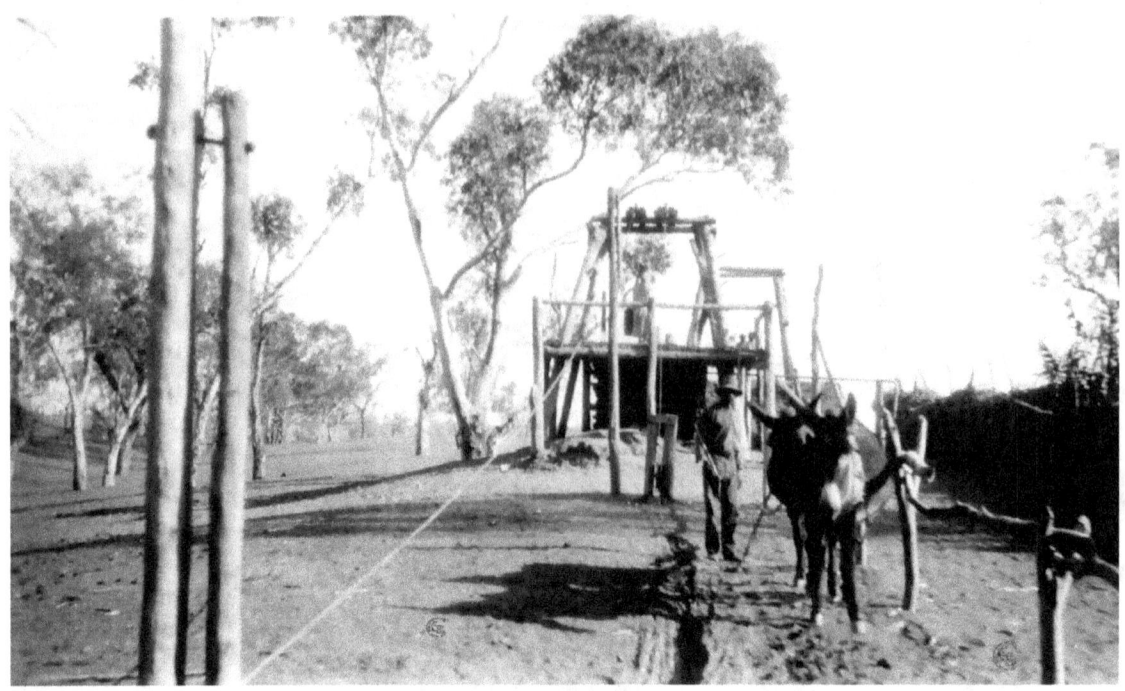

The same as a 'Camel Whip' but using mules, at Stuarts Well, south of Alice Springs

The structure on the right of the photo is a Bush Yard, simply made by piling up trees and branches to hold stock on an overnight stop.

Water was drawn from the well using a large bucket pulled up by the mules, and tipped into a chute which fed the water into a stock-trough inside the yard. Payment was so much per hundred head of stock.

More Mules

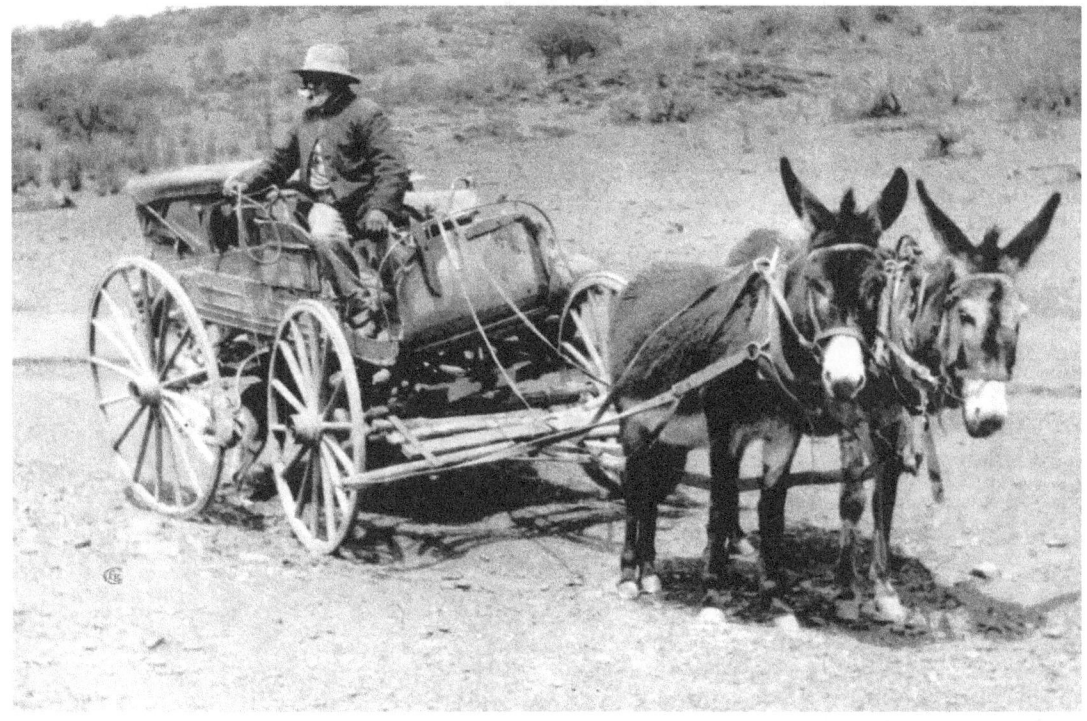

Passing traffic on the road from Parachilna to Blinman in the Flinders Ranges, South Australia. My father titled this photo, "Yellow Cab Sir."

I just wish that he had parked his car elsewhere though. Maybe I'll use some photo-magic tricks one day to remove it.

But not the 'kangaroo dog' hiding under the buggy to get out of the sun!

Poepples Corner 1

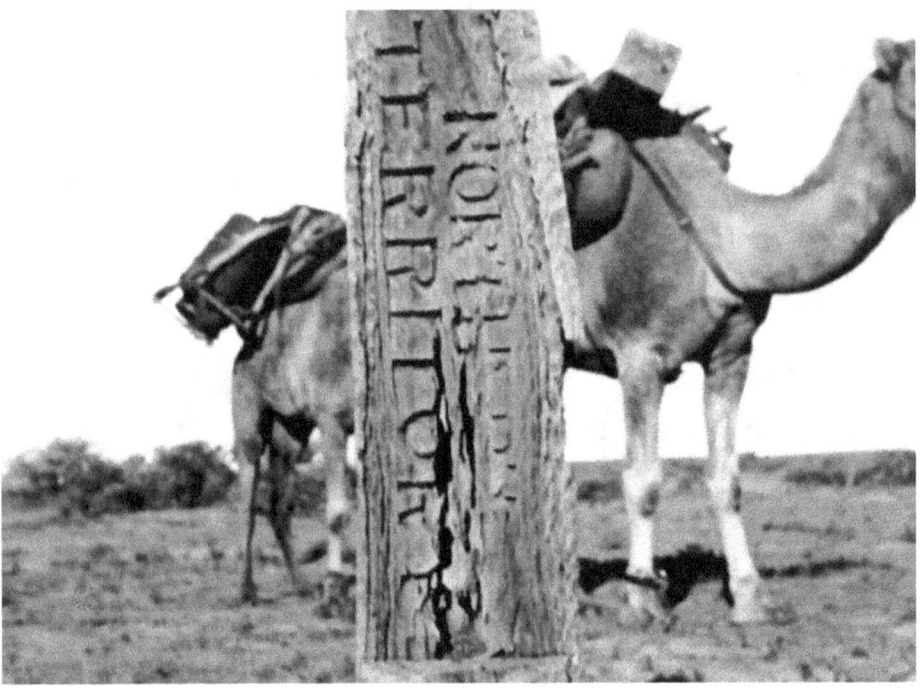

Poepples corner, where the Northern Territory, Queensland and South Australia meet in the Simpson Desert. The photo above was taken by Bob Rumball after a camel ride from Dalhousie Springs in 1927, and the one below many years later...But it's the same post!

It has been replaced with a new post, but the original is now stuck in a block of concrete in a museum. I apologize for the quality of the photo below, but it's the only one I could find of the original post, apart from mine. But it is interesting to note the different method of travel.

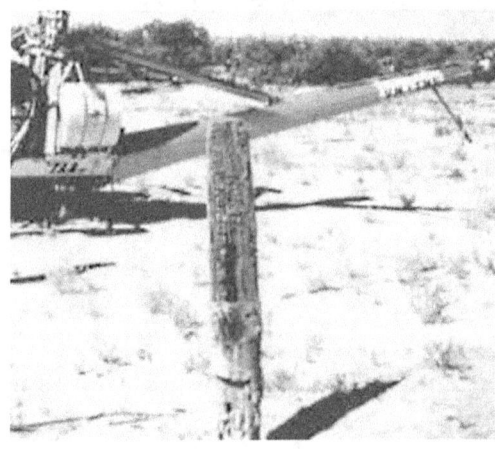

Poepples Corner 2

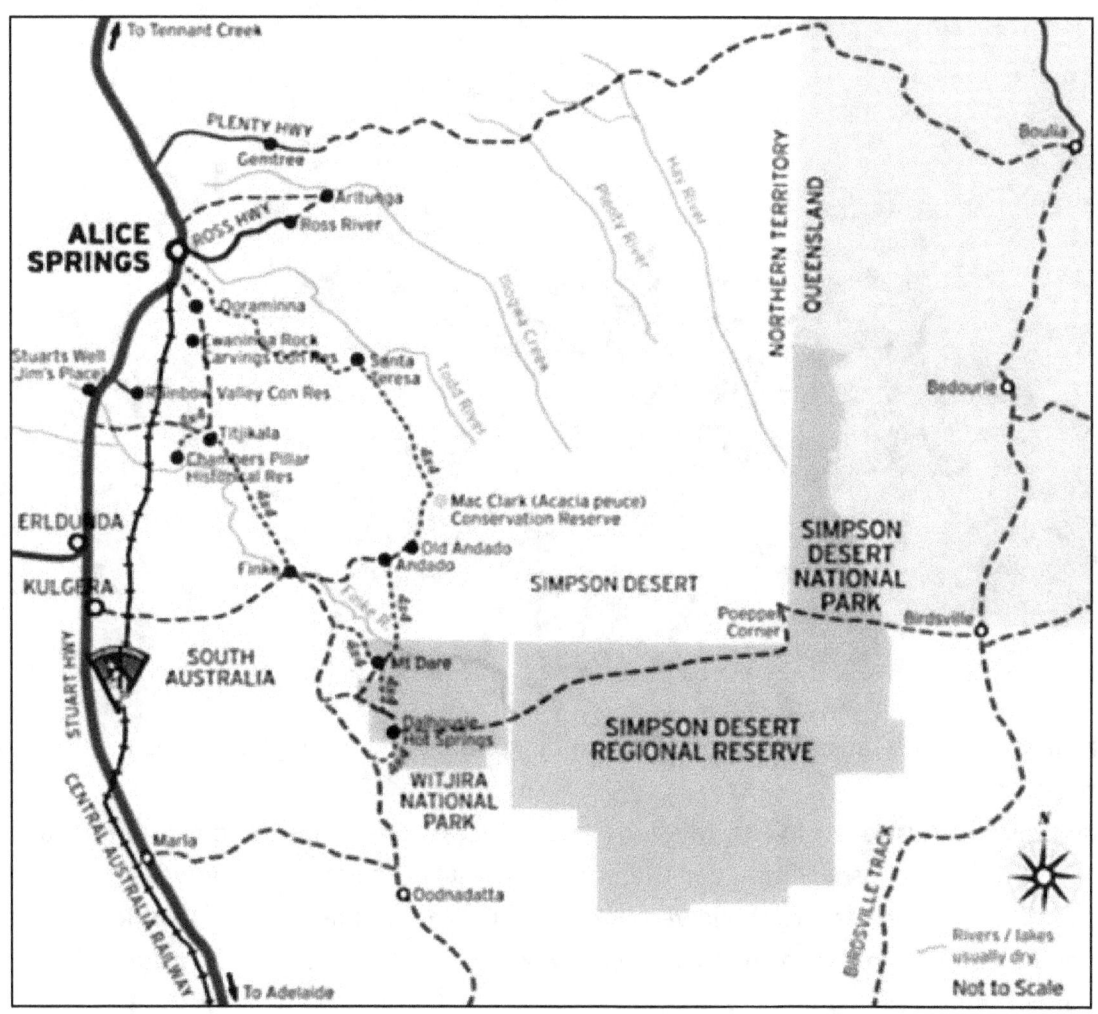

A recent map showing Poepples Corner.
Note the Finke River from Chambers Pillar to Finke (the town).

It is along the western side of this stretch of river that the Depot Sand-hills are. The old Ghan rail line was much closer to the river in the old days, and fine, red drift sand often covered the rails in spite of corrugated iron shields placed close to the rails.

Every one, passengers and all, would get out and clear the sand off to allow the train to proceed.

Todd Street Alice Springs 1929

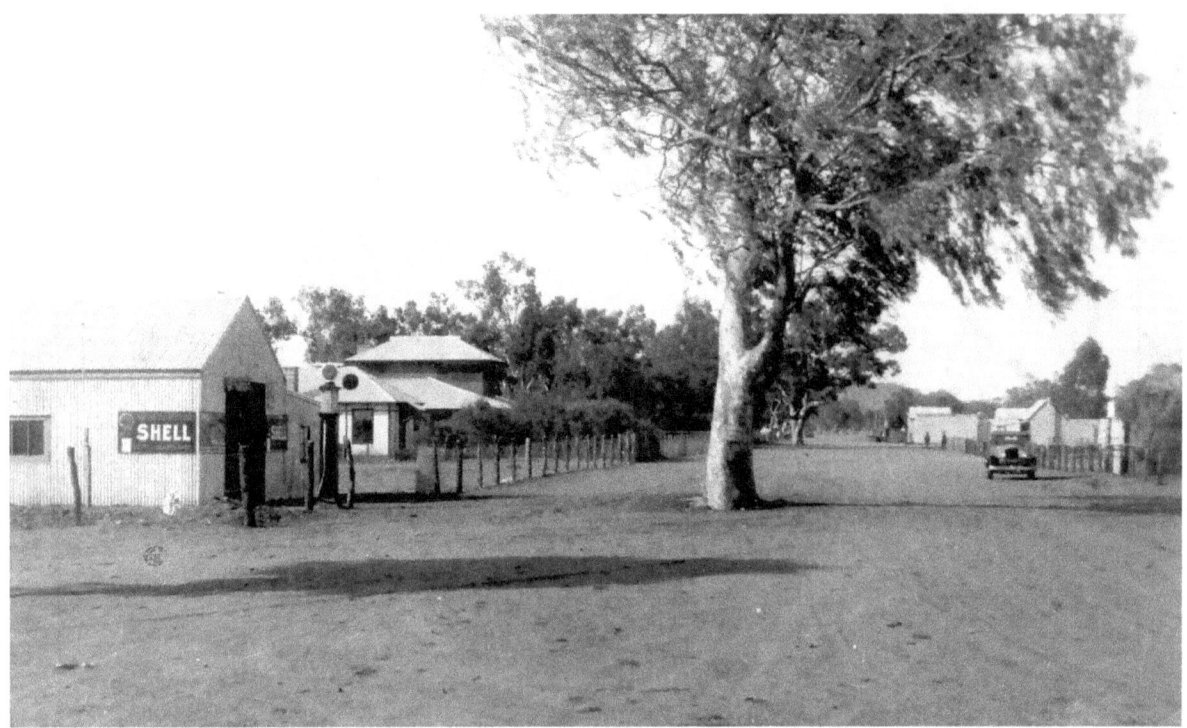

All the buildings in this photo have long since gone. All excepting the two-story building on the left.

That was the Australian Inland Mission hostel. It was a very special building in that it was designed by John Flynn specifically for the outback climate. The thick stone walls, cellar and the 'lantern top' above the main roof allowed hot air to rise and escape. Natural ventilation drew the cooler air upwards from the cellar. This process was assisted by a system of air ducts through-out the building.

Built in 1926 and known then as 'Adelaide House', the building is now used as a museum. The lowset house alongside was the Presbyterian Manse which was moved further back on the block of land and the Flynn Church built there; opened in 1956 by Prime Minister Bob Menzies.

The author and his wife were the first married in the church. Aileen had been a radio operator for the Flying Doctor Service, started by John Flynn.

Thank You

Thanks for buying my "Camels in the Aussie Outback" the Paper-back version.

The book has been previously published as a Kindle eBook, but this version has a few more photos and stories.

The 8 inch by 10 inch size gives more room to present a good high resolution at a respectable size.

The Kindle version is being updated to reflect the changes made in this version.

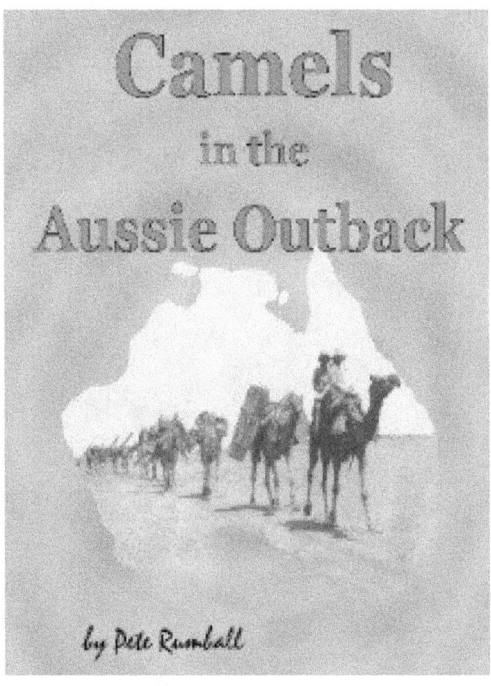

www.ingramcontent.com/pod-product-compliance
Lightning Source LLC
Chambersburg PA
CBHW081757170526
45167CB00009B/4052